A STUDENT'S GUIDE TO
LITERATURE

THE PRESTON A. WELLS JR.
GUIDES TO THE MAJOR DISCIPLINES

EDITOR
Jeremy Beer

⁂

PHILOSOPHY   *Ralph M. McInerny*

LITERATURE   *R. V. Young*

LIBERAL LEARNING   *James V. Schall, S.J.*

THE STUDY OF HISTORY   *John Lukacs*

THE CORE CURRICULUM   *Mark C. Henrie*

U.S. HISTORY   *Wilfred M. McClay*

ECONOMICS   *Paul Heyne*

POLITICAL PHILOSOPHY   *Harvey C. Mansfield*

PSYCHOLOGY   *Daniel N. Robinson*

CLASSICS   *Bruce S. Thornton*

AMERICAN POLITICAL THOUGHT   *George W. Carey*

RELIGIOUS STUDIES   *D. G. Hart*

THE STUDY OF LAW   *Gerard V. Bradley*

NATURAL SCIENCE   *Stephen M. Barr*

A Student's Guide to Literature

R. V. YOUNG

ISI BOOKS

WILMINGTON, DELAWARE

A Student's Guide to Literature is made possible by grants from the Lee and Ramona Bass Foundation, the Huston Foundation, Barre Seid Foundation, and the Wilbur Foundation. The Intercollegiate Studies Institute gratefully acknowledges their support.

Young, R. V., 1947–

A student's guide to literature / R. V. Young. —Wilmington, Del. : ISI Books, 2000.

p. ; cm.
(Preston A. Wells Jr. guides to the major disciplines)
ISBN: 978-1-882926-40-4 ; 1882926404
1. Literature—History and criticism. I. Title. II. Series.

PN 524 .Y68 2000   99091150
809—dc21

ISI Books
Post Office Box 4431
Wilmington, DE 19807-0431

Cover and Interior Design by Sam Torode

CONTENTS

INTRODUCTORY NOTE:
THE PARADOX OF LITERATURE

❦

L ITERATURE IS PARADOXICAL both in its nature and in its effect upon readers. Although letters inscribed upon a page or the words of a spoken utterance are the media of a literary work, the work itself is neither the ink and paper nor the oral performance. A successful poem or story compels our attention and seizes us with a sense of its reality, even while we know that it is essentially (even when based upon historical fact) something made up—a fiction. The most memorable works of literature are charged with significance and cry out for understanding, reflection, interpretation; but this meaning carries most conviction insofar as it is *not* explicit—not paraded with banners flying and trumpets blaring. "We hate poetry that has a palpable design upon us," says John Keats.[1] The role of literature in society is similarly equivocal. It can be explained simply as entertainment or recreation; men and women have always told stories and sung songs to amuse themselves, to pass the time, to lighten the burdens of "real life." At the same time, literature has assumed a central place in education and the transmission of culture throughout the history of Western civilization, contributing a sense of communal identity and shaping both individual and social understanding of human experience. The intimate part played by literature in cultural tradition has been a source of alarm to moralists and reformers from Plato to the media critics and multiculturalists of our own day.

Literature, then, must be approached both with caution and abandon. A primary purpose of the study of literature is to learn to read critically, to maintain reserve and distance in the face of an engaging, even beguiling, object. And yet, like any work of art—a symphony, for example, or a painting—a novel or an epic yields up its secrets only to a reader who yields himself to its power. It is for this reason that literary study is a humane or humanistic discipline, not an exact or empirical science. The ideal researcher in the physical sciences, insofar as he sticks rigorously to science, will be absolutely objective in the sense that his humanity will exert no influence on his methods or conclusions. Even a medical researcher will be interested in the human body only as a biological mechanism, not as the outward manifestation of a person with a soul. The literary scholar must of course be objective in the sense that he is disinterested; he must not have an individual or personal stake in the interpretation. And yet, although the critic's fate is not the fate of King

Lear, the critic's human sympathy with the plight of that tragic protagonist is part of his critical response to the play as literature. The human compassion of the cancer researcher for the victims of the disease, while it may be an important motive, is not part of his research, not an element in his science as such. The natural sciences, therefore, provide a very poor model for scholarship in the humanities. To be sure, there are factual, "scientific" elements of great importance to inquiry in all the arts: a knowledge of Elizabethan stagecraft and printshop practices can furnish a good deal of useful information about how *Hamlet* was seen by contemporaries and how the text was preserved, but such facts will never explain why the play is still moving and important. Works of literature are not natural phenomena or specimens; they are rather part of the cultural fabric of the world that we all inhabit. A poet, says William Wordsworth, "is a man speaking to men."[2] We cannot approach poets and poems as an entomologist approaches ants and ant hills.

Literature is vast and complex; a "guide" of this length can only be a modest sketch of the subject. My purpose is to provide a brief description of the nature and purpose of literature and some sense of how it may be best approached. I shall say something about the concept of literary kinds or genres, and something about how literature has developed along with the development of Western civilization. I shall not discuss the literature of other civilizations, principally because

I lack the competence, but also because I suspect that *literature* in the sense that I use the term, although no longer unique to the West, is a uniquely Western idea. Finally, I shall list some of the indispensable works of our tradition, of which every educated person should have some knowledge, as well as lesser works that are also very fine or very influential and well worth perusal. The list will not be comprehensive: this essay is intended not only for undergraduate literature majors, but for students of any age who wish to have a knowledge of literature commensurate with a baccalaureate degree. Nothing that I can say will take the place of simply reading these works, but I hope that this *Guide* will enable students to plan their own literary education, or fill in the gaps of such awareness as they possess, with confidence and prudence.

A STUDENT'S GUIDE TO LITERATURE

۰

THE FIRST PROBLEM one encounters in attempting to define the nature and purpose of literature is the ambiguity of the key terms. The word "literature" itself comprises a wide variety of sometimes incompatible meanings. Its etymological origin, the Latin word *littera*, means, like the English word "letter," both a graphic mark representing a sound or a missive or written communication. *Litteratura* in Latin, like "literature" in English and the corresponding cognate words in the various European vernacular tongues, had as its most important sense those writings which constitute the elements of liberal learning. Hence a *litteratus* was a man notable for knowledge and cultivation. This notion is the basis for the English phrase "a man of letters." "Literature" as a term for written works of art—what Wellek and Warren call "the literary work of art"[3]—is, however, a nineteenth-century development. The older generic term was "poetry," but today this word is applied almost exclusively to works written in verse rather than prose; that is, poetry deploys language measured off in metrical "feet," or at least divided into free verse lines. Hence, for much of this century, English departments have offered introductory courses and patronized introductory anthologies to "Literature," divided into units on "Poetry," "Fiction," and "Drama."

Although it was generally rejected as a substantial distinction by ancient and Renaissance criticism, the force of the prose/verse distinction has strengthened over the past two to three centuries because of the rise of prose fiction, which has taken over the business of telling stories and confined verse almost exclusively to lyrical and satirical modes. Narrative verse is rarely written now, and contemporary verse drama tends to have an air of artificiality. So far as I know, no one has written scientific exposition in verse since Erasmus Darwin (grandfather of the more famous Charles) published *The Botanic Garden* in heroic couplets late in the eighteenth century. Hence it makes sense in the twentieth century to regard short to moderate length lyrical, reflective, or satirical *poetry* as a particular kind of literature as distinguished from fiction and *drama,* which tell stories through narration and theatrical representation.[4] My own practice will be to alternate the terms "poetry" and "literature"; the latter is the more common usage today, while the former will serve as a reminder that it is *imaginative* literature that is under discussion.

The account of literature given here will rest upon the ancient assumption of Plato and Aristotle that the essence of literature, or poetry, is **mimesis**; that is, the **imitation** or **representation** of reality or the human experience of reality. Whether this fundamental element of literature is cause for the disapproval of Socrates in Plato's *Republic* or for Aristotle's approval in the *Poetics,* the mimetic function of literature is generally taken for granted by classical thinkers. This basic fact is difficult to demonstrate precisely because it is the self-evident intuition of all mankind: when a friend has just read a new novel or seen a new movie, our first question is, "What is it about?" We expect, above all, a description of the characters as they act and relate to one another. We wish to know what this particular work shows us about how life is lived. As a representation of reality, a work of literature is an object *made* by an author. Our word "poet" comes from the Greek verb *poieo,* "to make." Our word "fiction" is similarly derived from the Latin *Ingo,* "to fashion," "to

----

HOMER, it is now generally agreed in accordance with ancient tradition, composed the *Iliad* and the *Odyssey* around 700 B.C., drawing upon an oral tradition of poetic material handed down by memory. Probably a native of Chios or Smyrna, he may well have been blind (heroic oral poetry would be an obvious choice of career for a blind man in a warrior society), and some contemporary may well have written the poems down in the letters that the Greeks were just in the process of adopting from the Phoenicians.

feign," or "to form." All of these terms suggest that at the center of literature or poetry is a verbal creation, made or formed to imitate or feign some aspect of the human experience of life.

To a remarkable extent, the categories devised by Aristotle in the *Poetics* to analyze tragedy are applicable, *mutatis mutandis,* to all the genres of literature. The **plot** *(mythos)* or story or arrangement of incidents is the primary element, because, he maintains, while character makes men what they are, it is action that

---

VIRGIL (PUBLIUS VERGILIUS MARO, 70–19 B.C.), was born into the landed gentry near Mantua, and, after receiving the standard rhetorical education of the day, he declined to become a pleader in the courts of law and pursued philosophical studies under the Epicurean Siro at Naples. His father's land was expropriated for distribution to veterans of Octavian's army in the aftermath of the Civil Wars, and tradition holds, somewhat implausibly, that *Eclogues* I celebrates the restoration of these lands by the man who would be Virgil's imperial patron as a result of the intercession of the poet's friends. There is no doubt that Virgil enjoyed the friendship, as well as the patronage, of the Emperor's advisor and confidant, Maecenas, who brought him to the attention of his master. Although Virgil was thus a court poet, the grim account of the human cost of Aeneas's quest to lay the foundation of the Roman Empire and the pervasive melancholy of the *Aeneid* suggest that the poem is hardly an uncritical celebration of imperialism. According to Boswell, Dr. Johnson "often used to quote, with great pathos," lines from Virgil's *Georgics* (III.66–68), which sadly recount how wretched man's best days slip through his fingers, and he is undone by sickness, age, labor, and ruthless death. Virgil is propagandist for no political platform.

determines happiness and unhappiness. The second, closely related element is **characterization** *(ethos),* which determines how individuals will act. **Diction** *(lexis)* or language or, best, **style** is the next element; it is closely related to **thought** *(dianoia)* or **themes** or ideas that emerge in the discourse. The final two elements, **spectacle** *(opsis)* and **music** *(melopoiia)* or **song** are, in the strict sense, specific features of ancient Greek tragedy, but even here we can find parallels in other genres. The "special effects" and the "sound track" are obvious corollaries from modern films, but even purely literary genres can provide similarities: the careful evocation of the setting of Thomas Hardy's Wessex novels is indispensable to their effect and import, and "music" emerges both in the style and structure of Henry James's prose fiction and Tennyson's verse.

Because careful attention to these comparatively minor elements—precise, vivid diction, evocative representation of scenes, and compelling speech rhythms—is the key to literary impact, works of nonfiction that are distinguished for beautiful or lively style are often counted as literature and thus survive after their more pragmatic original function has ceased to interest. Lucretius's *De rerum natura* would be at most a footnote in the history of philosophy if it were merely an exposition of Epicureanism; however, its powerful imagery and the spell cast by the melody of its hexameter verse have assured its enduring significance as a poem. Similarly, many of Emerson's essays furnish a compel-

ling, literary experience of the life of the mind even
for readers who regard him as singularly defective as
a moralist, and one need not be a high-church Anglican to be enthralled by the prose of Donne's sermons.
There are also works that seem to be on the border of
literature and some other discipline from the outset.
Plato's dialogues are the indispensable foundation of
Western philosophy, but some of the dialogues—the
Symposium, for instance, and the *Phaedrus* seem to
work as effectively as dramatic literature. The interpretation of Saint Thomas More's *Utopia* hinges, to
a large extent, on whether it is treated as a treatise in

HORACE (QUINTUS HORATIUS FLACCUS, 65–8 B.C.),
son of a freed slave who prospered, came from more modest origins than his friend Virgil. Nonetheless, his father had him well
educated at Rome and then Athens, where he was induced to
join the army of Brutus, whose defeat and suicide at Philippi are
so dramatically rendered by Shakespeare in *Julius Caesar.* With
his father's property mostly confiscated upon his return, Horace
secured a place in the Roman civil service. His poetry came to
the attention of Maecenas, who soon won for him the patronage of the forgiving Emperor Augustus. Horace's disposition is
the opposite of his melancholy comrade Virgil. Throughout his
poetry—whether in the wry wit of his *Satires* and *Epistles* or the
lyrical beauty of his Odes—Horace evinces a tolerant, detached
skepticism and good humor. He was pleased to accept the bene-
factions of Augustus and Maecenas, but he resisted their efforts
to involve him in politics or government. Preferring the leisure
of the Sabine farm that his poetry made famous, Horace's most
important bequest to European poetry is the theme of the superi-
ority of rural retirement to the ambitious life of court or city.

political philosophy or a work of literature. This does not mean that the distinction between fiction and nonfiction, between a poem and a treatise, is negligible; it simply means that there is a broad grey area at the border. We know the difference between day and night, but a long period of dusk makes it difficult to say when one ends and the other begins.

At the center of imaginative literature or poetry, then, is *mimesis* or *imitation:* the representation of human life—or more precisely, the representation of human experience. We are naturally curious creatures, but not merely in the manner of cats and monkeys; our specifically *human* curiosity is inspired by our consciousness—our awareness of the world around us and of our selves as situated within it. This self-consciousness necessarily entails a recognition of other selves, other souls. The poet is important because, by expressing himself, he opens up to us the mind and heart of another, and the knowledge of our likeness and difference from others is essential for our self-realization. The individual can only be defined—indeed, can only exist—in relation to other individuals. Thus while literature is the self-expression of the author, it is also the representation of the reader. A uniquely personal vision representing nothing save the bard's own genius would fail to be intelligible as literature; by the same token, a purely subjective reading, which ignores the structural and generic features of a work, which pays no heed to the intention inscribed in its intrinsic verbal substance, would fail to be an interpretation of the work itself. Literature—like the language from which it emerges—presupposes a communal culture, which in turn rests upon a common human nature.

The knowledge of human nature and the human condition that literature yields is the basis of its educational role. A poet or a novelist contributes to the moral and social formation of his readers less by providing moral precepts or lessons in citizenship than by shaping the moral imagination. Literature, then, is less concerned to assert what is right and wrong than to evoke the experience of good and evil. Shakespeare does not tell us that Edmund, in *King Lear,* is evil. Instead, he unfolds the layers of his villain's arrogance and self-pity, of his ambition and envy; and he allows him to make claims upon both our sympathy and fascination. Such is the peril of literature: one may choose to ignore the import of the drama as a whole and accept Edmund's claim to be a victim. A character on a grander scale of wickedness—the Satan of Milton's *Paradise Lost*—is notorious for having attracted the favor of romantically inclined readers from Blake and Shelley to William Empson. But if poetry is more dangerous than precept, it is also more powerful and engaging. The reader or theatrical spectator who has felt the full impact of *King Lear* has a knowledge more profound and moving than the simple proposition that deceit, betrayal, and murder are never justified; he will gain an emotional and imaginative revulsion at evil dressed up in bland excuse and political pretext. He will have an inner resistance to collaboration with the Edmunds he meets in the world, or to complicity with the Edmund who lurks within each of us.

"Poets aim either to teach or delight," is Horace's famous dictum in *The Art of Poetry,* and Sir Philip Sidney refines the saying by suggesting that teaching and delighting are bound up with one another: "But it is that fayning notable images of vertues, vices, or

---

OVID (PUBLIUS OVIDIUS NASO, 43 B.C.–A.D. 17), lacked the discretion (or the connections or the luck) of Virgil and Horace, who could maintain both their independence and the favor of the emperor. Ovid's early erotic poetry, its sensuality salted by witty self-mockery, seems designed to provoke respectable opinion. About the time Virgil's posthumous *Aeneid*, with its sombre portrayal of patriotic self-sacrifice, is appearing to universal acclaim, Ovid is suggesting that the seducer of another man's wife, when he breaks down her door, outwits rivals, and engages in a "night attack," is also a soldier in love's war (*Amores* I.ix). This classical version of "Make love, not war!" was bound to infuriate Augustus, whose imperial program demanded a restoration of the patriotism and chastity of the ancient Republic; when Ovid was involved in a scandal at court—possibly involving the Emperor's notoriously promiscuous granddaughter—Augustus banished him for life to the howling wilderness of Pontus, on the Black Sea at the edge of the Empire. Ovid's grand, quasi-epic retelling of Greek myth in the *Metamorphoses* and his celebration of Roman religious holidays in the *Fasti* were of no avail. His final poems, the *Ex Ponte* and the *Tristia*, are versified pleas for clemency that met with stony silence from Augustus and his successor, Tiberius. Rome's gayest and most charming poet died in miserable exile.

what els, with that delightfull teaching, which must be the right describing note to know a Poet by...."[5] Neither Horace nor Sidney is altogether free of the "sugar-coated-pill" theory of literary teaching; but, as the quotation from the latter suggests, their best instincts tell them that the morality in poetry is built into the poetic essence as such: "[the] fayning notable images of vertues, vices, or what els" *is* the poetry. As Sidney stresses, the power of literature to teach is bound up with its power to represent the human experience of life, but life as it has meaning for us. "Right Poets," he says, are like "the more excellent" painters, "who, hauing no law but wit, bestow that in cullours vpon you which is fittest for the eye to see: as the constant though lamenting looke of *Lucrecia,* when she punished in her selfe an others fault; wherein he painteth not *Lucrecia* whom he neuer sawe, but painteth the outwarde beauty of such a vertue."[6] Literature moves us by uniting goodness and beauty in our imagination; it seeks truth by means of fiction.

In assessing the representational element in literature, it is important always to bear in mind that, excepting drama, it is all done with words. Imaginative literature puts enormous pressure on language, with the salutary result of expanding, enriching, and refining the resources of that most characteristic yet remarkable of human traits. It is difficult to conceive of men and women without speech; hence we must think of language less as a human achievement than as a necessary condition of humanity. Speech, however, can develop or degenerate: among numerous other factors, the splendor of Shakespearean drama is in part the result of a tremendous growth in the power and subtlety of the English language in the course of the fifteenth and sixteenth centuries. But the writing and reading of poetry are a cause of linguistic burgeoning as well as an effect. Poetry is speech at its most intense: it requires all the resources of meaning and expression that a language can provide, but it also contributes to the creation of those resources. It would thus be difficult to determine whether the decline of Latin literature in late antiquity and the early Middle Ages resulted from a loss of complexity and refinement in the Latin language, or the language deteriorated because the poetry that was being written became cruder and less

———————

DANTE ALIGHIERI (1265–1321), was born in Florence, but exiled in 1301 as the result of a political vendetta while he was serving on an embassy to the pope in Rome. An idealist in politics as well as love, Dante steadfastly refused to make the admissions or concessions that would win him a reprieve, and so he never set foot in his native city again. *The Divine Comedy* is the work of an exile who knew the bitter taste of another man's bread and the wearying steepness of his stairs (*Paradiso* XVII.58–60). Dante was thus supremely fitted to recognize that life on this earth is exile, our true home in heaven. In Florence's storied Santa Croce Church, which holds the remains of luminaries such as Michelangelo, Machiavelli, Galileo, and Rossini, there is an empty tomb and monument for Dante, who lies buried, still an exile, in Ravenna.

imaginative. What can be said with certainty is that the study of literature requires the study of language, and that a knowledge of any language finally depends upon an acquaintance with the literature in which a language finds its most thoughtful and vital articulation. To be able to read critically, reflectively, and confidently requires wide reading in the great literature that has formed the linguistic culture of a society; and eloquent writing requires *a fortiori* a command of the most powerful resources of a language, which are only available, again, in its most important literature.

The interrelationships among literatures of different languages, cultures, and ages define the critical relationship between history and literature. Although a poet is inevitably affected by the social and political setting in which he writes, the crucial context of his work is the history of literature itself. Whatever the personal motives or public pressures that act upon a writer, the definitive goal of his efforts is, recognizably, a work of literature. Swift never actually admits that *A Modest Proposal* is a satire and not an actual scheme for using Irish infants as a foodstuff, and he never confesses that Lemuel Gulliver is a made-up character whose *Travels* were spun out of Swift's own fertile fantasy. Likewise, Thomas More appears to guarantee the authenticity of Raphael Hythlodaeus's account of a distant, perfectly ordered state by introducing himself as an uncomfortable auditor into the text of *Utopia*. Only the most naïve reader, however, would doubt for a moment that these works are fictions, created by their authors to respond to and take their place among the poems and stories of other authors. The relationship of literature to actual history—including an author's own biography—is always important, but always oblique. For this reason, the place of literature in education is unique. It involves a good deal of historical knowledge of persons, places, facts, dates, and the like; but these matters are, finally, ancillary to the study of literature per se, which dwells in the realm of the human spirit. Even as a particular poem is a structure of tension between author and reader, between a unique verbal form and the literary and linguistic conventions that constitute its matrix, just so is literature itself (like all creations of the mind) an institution within but not wholly of the flux of human history.

———

GEOFFREY CHAUCER (CA. 1340–1400), was born into a family of prosperous wine merchants, but by virtue of good education and innate gifts, he came to be on familiar terms with nobles and kings. As a young man he was a courtly lover and a soldier, taken prisoner by the French and subsequently ransomed in the Hundred Years' War. In his later years, he worked as a diplomat and a civil servant and enjoyed the patronage of John of Gaunt as well as both Richard II and Henry IV. His masterpiece, *The Canterbury Tales*, is the fruit of a lifetime rich in experience and observation of humanity. The surface tone of the work is a detached, tolerant, and good-humored skepticism, yet there is nothing cynical in Chaucer, whose work bespeaks not only wisdom but an abiding sympathy for his fellow man born of a profound charity.

The history of literature is thus best pursued in terms of the emergence, development, and transformation of **genres** or literary "kinds." The difficulty of this approach is that "genre," like "literature" itself, is an ambiguous term. There is more than one principle for dividing up literary works into categories, and the generally recognized genres that have emerged in the course of literary history are not always logically compatible. Most works draw on a variety of generic conventions, and practically no memorable work fits comfortably into the definitions offered by scholars—one of the marks of literary greatness is a testing of the conventional boundaries of the recognized genres. The conventions are not, therefore, irrelevant or unimportant. Even in "realistic" novels, we unconsciously accept impossibly knowledgeable and coherent narrative perspectives because the conventions of prose fiction are part of our literary culture. And it is those innovative authors who challenge or subvert the conventions that most depend upon them. Any reasonably literate person can work out the conventions of the Victorian novel in the course of reading, but it requires a high degree of critical sophistication—a conscious awareness that the usual means of story-telling have been discarded—to respond to the stream-of-consciousness narration of *To the Lighthouse* or the lack of a conventional plot in *Waiting for Godot*.

In the course of Western literary history, genres have developed in terms both of formal features and aspects of tone and content, and the same term can be used to specify either a closely defined literary form or a general theme or subject. Pure examples of specific genres are the exception rather than the rule. For example, much of the poetry of Robert Frost may reasonably be described as "pastoral," but he did not write formal pastorals on the model of Theocritus's *Idylls* or Virgil's *Eclogues* or strict Renaissance imitations like Petrarch's *Bucolicum carmen*. Indeed, many of the greatest literary achievements grow out of an author's re-imagining both the generic form and the spiritual vision of his great predecessors: for example, an "epic" novel—a prose narrative on a grand scale, like *Moby-Dick* or *War and Peace*—can be seen as a modernized version of the quest and conflict motifs of ancient epic as founded by Homer and Virgil. Genre, then, is an indispensable literary concept as it applies both to the form of individual works and to the historical unfolding of literary tradition; however, it would be foolish to bind particular poems, plays, and stories to generic models, as if they were so many beds of Procrustes. One way of regarding a work of literature is to see it as a result of a poet coming to terms with the conventions of his art and the limits of nature, while at the same time, in Sidney's grand phrase, "freely ranging onely within the Zodiack of his owne wit."[7] Or as T. S. Eliot says, literature represents a confrontation and convergence of "Tradition and the Individual Talent."[8]

At the fountainhead of Western literature is the

epic—the story of a hero struggling against the constraints of the human condition. Western literature—and in some measure Western culture and education—begins with the *Iliad* and the *Odyssey,* traditionally ascribed to the blind bard Homer, who probably put the poems in roughly their present form about seven centuries before the birth of Christ. Beginning in Athens and the other Greek city-states at least as early as the fifth century B.C., the epics of Homer have spread throughout the Western world and been a continuous influence upon culture, education, and literature even to the present day. Of course the same argument could be made about the opening books of the Bible, especially Genesis and Exodus, attributed to Moses. These books go back more than 1200 years before the birth of Christ, and they are certainly epic in their theme and scope and in the grandeur of their style. The account

---

MIGUEL DE CERVANTES (1547–1616), lived a life plagued with misfortune. Heroic service in the Battle of Lepanto (1571), which turned the tide in Christendom's struggle against a growing Turkish threat, cost him his left eye and the use of his left arm. In 1575 he was captured by Barbary pirates and languished five long years in an Algerian prison before being ransomed. He spent the rest of his life eking out a meager living as a writer and minor government functionary. He was more than fifty when he attained his first success with the first part of *Don Quixote* (1605), and even this work and its glorious second part (1615) brought him little prosperity to match his fame. Cervantes, unlike Virgil and Horace, endured extremely ill fortune in patrons—the noblemen to whom he dedicated the first and second parts of

of the Hebrews' escape from slavery in Egypt and their conquest of the Promised Land, for instance, is an undeniably epic tale. The books of the Bible, however, have been preserved not as poetry, but rather as sacred history and revealed truth. Indeed, the survival of classical literature, with its idolatrous and often unedifying mythology, was possible in a severely Christian world largely because the attitude of the ancient Greeks and Romans toward their gods and the stories about them never involved the rigorous claims of truth that Christians and Jews attach to their Scriptures. Although the influence of the Bible on Western culture is thus as great as that of Homer and all of Greek and Roman literature combined, it is an influence of a different order. Until the last two or three centuries, almost no one would have thought of Exodus as "poetry" in the same way as the *Iliad*.

It is the *Iliad,* the tale of the wrath of Achilles in the tenth and final year of the Greek siege of Troy, and its companion piece, the *Odyssey,* which recounts the ten-year quest of the hero Odysseus to return to his homeland, that define the characteristics of the epic for the Western literary tradition. These characteristics will be familiar to most students who have read a

---

his masterpiece, and who would otherwise be forgotten, were insensible to his genius and ignored him. The most influential work of Western fiction brought its author lasting fame, but no worldly success.

few fragments of the *Odyssey* or the *Divine Comedy* or *Paradise Lost* in a literature anthology. *An epic is a poem about a great quest or conflict that involves the destiny of nations. Its characters are of imposing stature—gods and heroes—its style is grand and dignified, its setting encompasses heaven and earth, and it deploys specific epic devices like the extended Homeric simile and the catalogue of warriors.* And so on. This standard description is certainly unexceptionable as far as it goes, but it leaves out the speed of the narration, the clean simplicity of the style ("grand" must not be allowed to suggest "heavy" or "stodgy"), the vivid humanity of the "heroic" characters, and above all the tight focus of the plot not on the fate of peoples, but on the passionate struggles of individual men and women. The *Iliad* picks up in the tenth year of the war and begins with tawdry quarrels over captive concubines. It ends not with the wooden horse and the sack of Troy, but with the brutal and tragic slaying of Hector and the sure knowledge that his conqueror Achilles will soon follow him to an early grave. The Odyssey likewise begins in medias res in the final year of the hero's quest, and its focus is on his very personal story: a man trying to come home after a war to be reunited with his wife and son. Homer has endured because he has told with surpassing beauty, but also with unflinching moral realism, stories that still resonate in our minds and hearts.

The Western world has produced three other epics that are essential to a liberal education. Virgil's *Aeneid,*

Dante's *Divine Comedy*, and Milton's *Paradise Lost*. Although Homer was the first epic poet, there can be no doubt that Virgil exerted a greater direct influence on the development of the literary tradition. After the gradual disintegration of the Roman Empire, Western Europe was generally ignorant of Greek, and Homer's works were known largely by report. Virgil, however,

---

WILLIAM SHAKESPEARE (1564–1616), undoubtedly wrote the plays attributed to him, and no more improbable substitute has been suggested than the current favorite, the feckless seventeenth Earl of Oxford, Edward de Vere. Most great writers are very intelligent, but they are usually not intellectuals, infrequently scholars, and very rarely aristocrats—Lord Byron and Count Tolstoy are in a decided minority. Shakespeare had all the education and experience he needed because he was, in Henry James's phrase, a man "on whom nothing was lost." He was almost certainly reared Catholic at a time of increasing persecution of the old faith on the part of Queen Elizabeth's government. A growing body of evidence suggests that he worked as a school master and journeyman actor in Catholic households in the North of England during the "lost years" of the later 1580s, and this lends some probability to the report (or accusation) by a late seventeenth-century Anglican clergyman that the playwright "died a papist." Shakespeare's plays and poems, especially his mysterious Sonnets (1609), may be safely assumed to grow out of his own experiences, interests, and longings; their actual relationship to his life, however, cannot be determined with any certainty. More than any other poet, Shakespeare created a secondary world of remarkable depth and richness in a theatre fittingly called the Globe. His works, analogous to the great work of creation itself, tell us unerringly that there is a creator behind them, but they reveal almost nothing of his inner being. It is difficult to ascertain how or why the world came into being,

was read throughout the Middle Ages and exercised an incalculable influence on an enormous variety of writers over the next 2,000 years down to our own day. In contrast to the *Iliad* and the *Odyssey,* the *Aeneid* is a reflective poem about a hero of self-renunciation. A reluctant warrior, "pius Aeneas" always pays reverence to the gods and to his destiny; he always does his duty. But while Virgil celebrates the triumphant origins of the grandeur that will be Rome, he also ruefully acknowledges the bitter anguish that bloody triumph costs. Virgil is so intensely aware of human limitations, so profoundly concerned with the spiritual trials of his hero, that it is no wonder that he was long regarded as half-Christian. That the central epic of the Western literary tradition is full of ambiguity and doubt about conquest and warfare suggests that European culture is less an unthinking exercise in triumphalist hegemony than many surmise.

---

yet impossible to imagine it not being, it is difficult to understand how anyone could have created Shakespeare's dramatic world, yet impossible to imagine it not being there.

The place of Virgil in Western literature and civilization is indicated by the next indispensable epic of that tradition: in the *Divine Comedy,* Dante takes the character "Virgil" as his mentor and guide through hell and purgatory during the first two-thirds of the poem. His understanding of literary style and his aspiration are shaped by the poet Virgil, and it is Dante's explicit intention to join Virgil and his classical predecessors in the exclusive circle of culture-defining poets and philosophers. As Homer is taken to be an expression of the Greek heroic age and Virgil of the Roman Empire, so Dante is often read and taught as the embodiment of the medieval worldview, and especially of the Thomistic theological synthesis. Naturally, there is an element of truth in these propositions, but they

---

JOHN DONNE (1572–1631), son of Saint Thomas More's great niece and with two Jesuit uncles, was reared as a Catholic recusant ("refuser") in a time of increasing persecution. His bold and witty early love poems, as well as his satires, were a provocation to Protestant respectability in Elizabethan England in the same fashion that Ovid affronted respectable society in Augustan Rome. Donne, whose personae in his love poems often assume the pose of a cynical seducer, threw away all his worldly prospects to elope with the seventeen-year-old daughter of a wealthy country gentleman. After ten years of poverty on the margins of Jacobean society, Donne found a way to reconcile his conscience with membership in the Church of England. He became a clergyman and eventually Dean of St. Paul's Cathedral. His spiritual struggles produced some of the most powerful devotional poetry in English, and his sermons and *Devotions upon Emergent Occasions* are among the glories of English prose.

are still superficial clichés. Dante's *Comedy* is certainly a vivid depiction of many aspects of his world—political, religious, social—and it brings to the fore both the philosophical outlook he derived from the thinkers of his era (including Saint Thomas Aquinas) and his bitter personal experience. But the poem is above all a dramatization of a man's self-discovery and quest for salvation—the restoration of that self. His journey involves the confrontation with sin, the experience of penitence, and the glory of reconciliation with God. The terms of the poem are irreducibly Christian, and it is otherwise unintelligible; however, the Christian account of the human situation is sufficiently resonant to adherents of other religions or of no religion at all for Dante's poem to engage their intellects and touch their hearts. In the course of creating in the Tuscan vernacular a style to challenge Virgil's Latin, Dante, with his younger contemporary Petrarch, laid the groundwork of the modern Italian language. In this feat is manifest the intimate and essential relationship between language and literature, which was so significant to Renaissance humanism: by the act of literary creation a language and thus a culture achieves a kind of permanence and ideal realization. As it becomes the Esperanto of the global marketplace, English is showing the same wear and tear and debasement that Latin suffered in the later imperial era. Yet as long as the works of Shakespeare and other great English writers are available, the genius of the language—its responsiveness to the powers of imagination—will remain.

One of the writers who expanded the capacities of the English language is John Milton, author of the

---

JOHN MILTON (1608–74), was a truly learned poet in academic terms, who also traveled widely and was directly involved in the most important political and religious affairs of his day. His major works are, predictably, learned and overtly engaged with the leading issues of his society. The case of Milton shows us the kind of works that the "unlearned" Shakespeare would have produced had he enjoyed the extensive formal education and worldly advantages that disdainers of "the man from Stratford" think he should have had in order to write his plays and sonnets—which in fact are rather popular and earthy in tone and style in contrast to Milton's highly intellectual and scholarly poetry. Milton in fact displays all the perversity of a radical intellectual. His Christmas poem, "On the Morning of Christ's Nativity," virtually ignores the tenderness and affectivity of the manger scene and compares the Baby Jesus to the serpent-strangling infant Hercules in what has been called an "epic Christmas carol." In *Comus* Milton uses the masque—a genre notorious as a pretext for song, dance, sumptuous costumes, and elaborate stage sets—as a vehicle for the exposition of an austere Christian Neoplatonism. Although he was the most important poet of the seventeenth century, Milton devoted his prime middle years to political and religious controversy in prose. He won the admiration of Puritans by attacking the liturgy and episcopal hierarchy of the Church of England and lost it by supporting the legalization of divorce (Milton's first marriage, to a seventeen-year-old royalist, was not a happy one). His vigorous defense of the execution of Charles I favorably impressed Cromwell, and the poet served for a number of years in the Lord Protector's Interregnum government. It was only after the Restoration of Charles II and the bishops of the Church of England, when Milton had lost his

last great Western epic. In Milton, as in Dante, the influence of Virgil is prominent, and the closest a reader of English can get to the verbal "feel" of the epic hexameters of the *Aeneid* without reading it in Latin is to read the blank verse of *Paradise Lost.* There is no poem in English that better exemplifies the heroic dignity of the grand style, and it is one of the paradoxes of literature that one language can be served so well by bending it to the imperatives of another. It is the measure of Milton's insight and taste that he so unerringly knows exactly how far he can craft English verse to the turns of Latinate diction and syntax in the pursuit of "Things unattempted yet in Prose or Rhime" (I.16). What Milton does with the thematic substance of epic is another paradox. *Paradise Lost* is, indisputably, a great epic poem of classical style and heroic scale, and yet it not only is the last epic; it may also be said to have finished off the epic. The epic catalogues are mostly lists of fallen angels; the character who is most consistently heroic in word and action and attitude is Satan. Most telling, the only epic battle in the entire poem—the War in Heaven in Book VI—is inconsequential and borders at times on the comic, since none of the angels are able to suffer serious injury, much less

political hopes, his standing in society, and even his eyesight that he wrote those works on biblical themes in classical form that established him among the world's greatest poets: *Paradise Lost, Paradise Regained*, and *Samson Agonistes*.

death, because of their ethereal substance. Whether Milton is shaping a new vision of the heroic military virtues in terms of inner, spiritual strength or simply rejecting them is a question that scholars continue to debate. In any case, no one in the Western world has been able to write a genuine or unqualified epic since.

Of course there have been numerous important poems that make us think of epics: mock epics, like Dryden's *Mac Flecknoe* and *Absalom and Achitophel* and Pope's *Rape of the Lock* and *Dunciad,* apply epic conventions to the trivial or ridiculous with satiric intent. Romantic epics, like Wordsworth's *Prelude,* Byron's *Childe Harold's Pilgrimage* and *Don Juan,* and Whitman's *Song of Myself* (indeed, the entirety of *Leaves of Grass*) treat the subjective experience of their equivocal heroes in quasi-epic terms.

Among the many other ancient long poems that are worth whatever time a student can find for them, mention has been made already of Lucretius's *On the*

JOHN BUNYAN (1628–88), was the son of a tinsmith who learned to read and write at a village school. A veteran of the Parliamentary Army during the Civil War, Bunyan joined a Nonconformist church in the 1650s and became a powerful Calvinist preacher. With the restoration of the monarchy and established church in 1660, unlicensed preaching became a crime, and Bunyan was jailed twice, the first time for more than twelve years. The fruit of the second of his imprisonments was *The Pilgrim's Progress*, an allegory of sin and redemption that has appealed to Christians of every persuasion.

Nature of Things, but the one indispensable poem among them all is Ovid's *Metamorphoses,* an elaborate retelling of a vast array of Greek myths involving change of form. The most important source of ancient mythology for medieval and Renaissance writers, the *Metamorphoses* is also a unique work of both sparkling sophistication and deep feeling. From the Middle Ages, the essential long work of poetry besides Dante's *Comedy* is Geoffrey Chaucer's *Canterbury Tales,* a collection of comic tales in rhyming couplets. Another remarkable collection of comic tales from the Middle Ages is Giovanni Boccaccio's prose *Decameron,* while Francois Rabelais's *Gargantua and Pantagruel* is an unclassifiable narrative, also in prose, which reflects the mischievous, satirical side of humanist learning also seen in Desiderius Erasmus's *Praise of Folly* and Thomas More's *Utopia.*

ALEXANDER POPE (1688–1744), was born a Roman Catholic in the year of the "Glorious Revolution" that expelled James II, put William III on the throne of England, secured the real sovereignty for Parliament, and ended any hope of a Catholic restoration. Although he consorted with skeptical rationalists and could have enjoyed numerous benefits (e.g., government sinecures) by nominally conforming to the established church, Pope remained true to his faith until his death. He suffered physical as well as religious disabilities: tuberculosis of the spine contracted as a child turned him into a hunchback who never grew much over four feet tall. His chronic ill health produced his famous phrase, "This long disease, my life" (*Epistle to Dr. Arbuthnot,* 132). Pope compensated by becoming the first English author to

Drama is the most social or communal art, because the individual dramatist is altogether dependent upon a host of collaborators to see his work realized, and periods of great drama are understandably rare. There is no dispute about the origin of Western drama in festivals of Dionysius in Athens during the fifth century before the birth of Christ. The plays that have survived from that century—the tragedies of Aeschylus, Sophocles, and Euripides and the comedies of Aristophanes—are the first dramatic works of our tradition and they are arguably the best. Two millennia will pass before anything comparable emerges. It is late in the Renaissance, in the sixteenth and seventeenth centuries, that we come upon the next great wave of theatrical genius in England, France, and Spain. The greatest of these dramatists, certainly the greatest dramatist of all time and possibly the greatest writer, is William Shake-

---

earn a substantial living by publishing his work. The great success of his translation of the *Iliad* into heroic couplets won him financial independence and retirement at a modest rural estate. Pope's heroic couplets are often regarded as the poetic expression of Enlightenment rationalism, but, as William Wimsatt decisively demonstrates, rhyme is inherently antirationalist in its juxtapositioning of words on the basis of sound alone. Pope's work has more in common with the poetry of wit of the sixteenth and seventeenth centuries than with the cool skepticism of a Voltaire or Diderot. It is not surprising, therefore, that Pope eschewed the symmetrical formalism of French gardens at his Twickenham estate in favor of the "natural" garden that foreshadowed Romanticism.

speare. Ideally, every English-speaking student should read all of his plays and poems, but a bare minimum would include the second *Henriad (Richard II, 1* and *2 Henry IV,* and *Henry V),* a selection of his mature romantic comedies (*The Merchant of Venice, As You Like It, Twelfth Night),* his late romance, *The Tempest,* and the greatest of the tragedies: *Romeo and Juliet, Hamlet, Othello, King Lear, Macbeth,* and *Antony and Cleopatra.* Among Shakespeare's English contemporaries, Christopher Marlowe's *Dr. Faustus* and at least a few of Ben Jonson's comedies—for example, *Volpone* and *The Alchemist*—should not be missed. Seventeenth-century France boasts its great triumvirate: the tragedians Corneille and Racine and the comedian Moliere. For Corneille, *Le Cid* is the obvious choice; for Racine, *Andromache* or *Phaedra;* for Moliere, *The Misanthrope* or *Tartuffe.* Spanish Golden-Age drama—the theatre of Cervantes' contemporaries—is an undiscovered treasure for most Americans. Lope de Vega is notable for his prodigious fecundity rather than for any one outstanding play. His younger contemporary, Calderon de la Barca, was also remarkably productive, but his *Life Is a Dream* stands out as perhaps the most powerful and representative baroque drama, while *The Prodigious Magician* is a fascinating version of the Faust legend. Tirso de Molina is known for one extremely powerful and influential play, *The Joker of Seville and the Dinner Guest of Stone,* the earliest theatrical treatment of the Don Juan legend.

Claims may be made for Congreve during the period of the Restoration and for Sheridan, Beaumarchais, and Schiller during the eighteenth century, but the one indisputable dramatic masterpiece since the Renaissance is Goethe's *Faust.* Perhaps more of a dramatic epic than a conventional stage play, *Faust* is probably the greatest single work of Romanticism and of German literature. Its place at the summit of world literature results from its unique blend of stylistic power, dramatic characterization, and philosophical depth and sophistication. Norway's Henrik Ibsen is probably the indispensable dramatist at the beginning of the modern period, but claims could be made for George Bernard Shaw, Bertolt Brecht, Samuel Beckett, Eugene Ionesco, and Luigi Pirandello.

The dominant literary form of the twentieth century is prose fiction, especially the novel. Although it is by no means the earliest piece of extended prose fiction, the novel may be said to begin with Miguel de Cervantes's *Don Quixote,* written in the early seven-

---

SAMUEL JOHNSON (1709–84), was the son of a bookseller whose death in 1731 left his family in poverty before his son could finish his degree at Oxford. Sickly as a child and suffering ill health all his life after years of deprivation and failure, by dint of perseverance and intellectual effort Johnson made himself into the most important English man of letters of the later eighteenth century. He is famous not for a particular great work of literature, but for his overall achievement. He compiled the first dictionary of the English language (1755), was important in

teenth century, which defines itself precisely as a narrative of naturally explicable events among recognizable characters of everyday life, as opposed to the fantastic exploits and magical escapades of chivalric romance. The central character's generally futile efforts to dwell in the enchanted realm of unfettered fancy are thus instrumental in laying down the *realistic* boundaries of the workaday world in which this *new* form, the novel, typically takes place. The **realism** associated with the novel (and the short story) refers principally to the accurate and convincing evocation of the concrete features of an ordinary world inhabited by recognizable human beings. Even a science fiction novel (as opposed to a work of fantasy) attempts to create a plausibly factual world of the future by extrapolating from current scientific fact and theory. Works of fantasy—from *Beowulf* to *The Faerie Queene* to *The Lord of the Rings*—although they include purely imaginary features (enchanted lakes, dragons, elves) may, nonetheless, be works of powerful *moral* and *spiritual*

---

the development of the essay and periodical literature, wrote a number of fine poems and an engaging philosophical romance (*Rasselas*, 1759), collaborated with James Boswell on an important work of travel literature, produced an edition of Shakespeare (1765) that is a landmark in textual editing and interpretive commentary, and laid the foundation for literary biography in *The Lives of the Poets* (1779–81). Johnson is himself the subject of the greatest biography in English, Boswell's *Life of Johnson* (1791), which records his wit, wisdom, and deep compassion, often concealed by a gruff exterior.

realism. "Realism" in this latter sense is not, however, a strictly literary term denoting a generic characteristic. The genius of *Don Quixote* lies in its dwelling in the territory of rigorous realism while glancing continuously and longingly at the ideal kingdom of chivalric imagination, thus merging "realism" in its literary and moral senses.

Cervantes's most effective early disciples in the development of the novel as a realist genre were eighteenth-century Englishmen, and among their novels the most important are probably Daniel Defoe's *Robinson Crusoe,* Henry Fielding's *Tom Jones,* and Laurence Sterne's *Tristram Shandy.* The great age of the novel is the nineteenth century, and England again boasts a remarkable galaxy of fiction writers. At the

---

JANE AUSTEN (1775–1817), was the daughter of a clergyman of the Church of England. She never married and lived with her family throughout her apparently uneventful life, thus giving the lie to the notion that powerful writers must have wide experience of the world, extensive education, and deal with great events (she never mentions the French Revolution or Napoleon). Writing about the domestic affairs of the rural gentry and village shopkeepers and the marital aspirations of their daughters—"the little bit (two inches wide) of ivory on which I work with so fine a brush as produces little effect after much labor" is her own description of her literary métier Jane Austen captures a vision of ordinary life in society that is unsentimental, ironic, and morally acute. She is, as C. S. Lewis opines, less the mother of Henry James than the niece of Dr. Johnson—a classical mind in the age of Romanticism.

turn of the century Jane Austen created six exquisitely crafted comedies of manners that combine sparkling style, keen irony, and profound moral insight. *Pride and Prejudice* may have been displaced as the most important by *Emma* as the result of a flurry of excellent cinematic adaptations. *Among* the great victorian novels, Dickens's *David Copperfield, Bleak House,* and *Great Expectations*; Thackeray's *Vanity Fair*; George Eliot's *Middlemarch* and *Mill on the Floss*; and Trollope's *Barchester Towers* and *The Way We Live Now* would seem to be indispensable. In America, Melville's very long *Moby-Dick* and very short *Billy Budd* and Mark Twain's wonderful *Huckleberry Finn* are contemporaneous achievements. Whether Mary Shelley's *Frankenstein* and Nathaniel Hawthorne's *Scarlet Letter* should be classified as novels or gothic romances, they are both books that should not be missed. In France the three great nineteenth-century novelists are Victor Hugo, especially for *Les Miserables*, Honore de Balzac, especially for *Pere Goriot*, and Gustave Flaubert, especially for *Madame Bovarie*. But it may be Russia that has the strongest claim to have produced the greatest novels of all time in Leo Tolstoy's *Anna Karenina* and *War and Peace*, Fyodor Dostoyevsky's *Crime and Punishment* and *Brothers Karamazov,* and Ivan Turgenev's *Fathers and Sons.*

In England *Heart of Darkness* and other works by the transplanted Pole, Joseph Conrad, and the late novels of the transplanted American, Henry James, mark the beginning of the twentieth century. The three great names of "high modernist" fiction in the first half of the twentieth century are the Irishman James Joyce, the Frenchman Marcel Proust, and the German Thomas Mann, whose characteristic works, *Ulysses, Remembrance of Things Past,* and *The Magic Mountain,* respectively, are marked by a preoccupation with alienated subjective consciousness and innovative technical virtuosity that renders their work very difficult—if not inaccessible—to most readers. Joyce's greatest disciple, and one of the greatest novelists of the twentieth century, is William Faulkner in works like *The Sound and the Fury* and *As I Lay Dying.* Yet the most enduring novelist of the early twentieth century, although she lacks academic cachet at the present, may be Sigrid Undset for her multivolume historical works, *Kristin Lavransdatter* and *The Master of Hestviken.* Perhaps no one comes closer to the great nineteenth-century Russians in achieving the esssential task of the novelist: to shape a complex, compelling narrative, peopled with convincing characters, and transfigured by profound spiritual significance.

SAMUEL TAYLOR COLERIDGE (1772–1834), who as a young man was a romantic visionary like his friend Wordsworth, was inspired by the French Revolution and the prospect of the imminent reform of the world. By the time their joint production, *Lyrical Ballads,* appeared in 1798, both men were growing disillusioned by the excesses of the Revolution and both would become increasingly conservative as they grew older. Coleridge's

It remains to mention the various genres of shorter poems: pastorals, satires, epigrams, and the lyric. While the extended narrative works—epic poetry and the novel—involve telling a story about various characters by means of a third-person narration, and drama by means of first-person dialogue among the characters, the typical shorter poem seems to be the utterance of the poet himself, speaking or singing his own thoughts or feelings. Certainly part of the power of both lyrical and satirical poetry is a sense of intimacy with the poet, of gazing through a window into a creative mind. This preoccupation with the actual, historical poet is, however, an illusion and a distraction from the poetry itself, which is always a fiction, always a representation. Once a poet has set about to *compose* a *poem* (something made), the sense of sincerity and spontaneity are part of the fiction. The poet is playing a role, assuming a voice, creating a persona, even if the

---

chief contribution to *Lyrical Ballads*, "The Rime of the Ancient Mariner," is among the most remarkable poems in English, but by 1802 he was lamenting the loss of his poetic powers in "Dejection: An Ode," a paradoxically splendid poem on the inability to write poetry. Coleridge's muse was in fact departing, as he slid into despondency over his unhappy marriage to Sarah Fricker and his futile love for Wordsworth's sister-in-law. His life was also bedeviled for many years by addiction to opium, which he began taking for medicinal purposes. He compensated for his failing powers as a poet by becoming the greatest English literary critic since Johnson. *Biographia Literaria* (1817) is his principal theoretical work.

poem has been inspired directly by his own *personal* experience. **Persona,** in Latin the mask worn by actors in Roman drama, is the literary term of art for precisely the "mask" or "countenance" the poet puts on and hides behind in order to provide a vehicle for the emotion and insight that must be detached from his own private experience in order to become part of ours. Hence even if someone discovers indisputable evidence of the identity of "Mr. W. H." or proves that there really was a "Dark Lady" in Shakespeare's actual life, these facts about the poet will not settle the interpretation of the poetry of the *Sonnets.*

Since the shorter poetic forms are even more dependent than drama and narrative on nuances of style, it is very difficult to get any sense of the power and beauty of translated lyrics, epigrams, or satires. A few poets are so critical to understanding the development of Western culture, not to say literature, that they must be known, even if only in translation. Among these I would include the surviving lyrics of Sappho, at least a few of the lyrics of Catullus, Ovid's *Amores,* and, above all, Petrarch's sonnets to Laura, which are crucial to our complex and equivocal ideas of sexual love even to this day. Equally important are the *Odes (Carmina)* of Horace, which are one of the principal sources of the idea of the virtuous, modest, but independent country life—a perennial theme in Anglo-American literature; his satires, which supply both the classic image of the inescapable bore and the earliest version of the Country

Mouse/City Mouse story; and the satires of Juvenal, which provide an influential condemnation of corrupt urban life, the idea of the "Vanity of Human Wishes" (in Dr. Johnson's English adaptation), and the telling satirist's phrase, "savage indignation."

There are many beautiful medieval lyrics, but the great tradition of the English lyric begins with Wyatt and Surrey early in the sixteenth century. Sidney's *Astrophil and Stella,* Spenser's *Amoretti* (along with his *Epithalamion*—the finest wedding song in any language), and Shakespeare's *Sonnets* are the best English sonnet sequences. The seventeenth century is a treasure trove of lyrical poetry. John Donne's *Songs and Sonets,* his *Satyres, Holy Sonnets,* and *Hymns* are at the

---

SIGRID UNDSET (1882–1949), was the daughter of a Norwegian archaeologist—a lineage which may in part account for the scrupulous historical accuracy of her treatment of medieval Norway in her historical fiction. Her life was marked by great sorrows, including divorce from her artist husband and the death of one of her sons in battle against the Nazis in the early stages of World War II; her novels give a generally grim view of human sinfulness and the struggle against passion. Undset's depictions of modern life are especially bleak, but her reputation rests on two massive fictional treatments of medieval Norway: the trilogy *Kristin Lavransdatter* (1920-22), and the tetralogy *The Master of Hestviken* (1925-27). It was after publication of the former that she was received into the Catholic Church in 1924. Undset was awarded the Nobel Prize (1928) largely on the basis of her historical novels, but her novels in modern settings are also fine works, and she was an excellent essayist on historical, social, and religious themes.

top of the list along with the "minor poems" of John Milton. Ben Jonson, Robert Herrick, and Andrew Marvell wrote exquisite lyrics and poems of reflection; George Herbert's *The Temple* is the finest collection of religious lyrics in English, but Crashaw's *Carmen Deo Nostro* and Henry Vaughan's *Silex Scintillans* are worthy successors. John Dryden, already mentioned as an author of mock epic, produced two of the best works of religiopolitical satire in *Religio Laici* and the very much underrated *The Hind and the Panther.* Dryden lays the foundation for the tremendous achievement in satire and mock epic of Alexander Pope, who dominates the eighteenth century.

The next great burst of lyrical poetry comes with the Romantic movement: Blake's *Songs of Innocence* and *Songs of Experience,* Coleridge's *Rime of the Ancient Mariner,* and the great odes of Shelley and Keats are among the most memorable of English poems. Wordsworth and Byron, mentioned for their variations on epic, also wrote many fine lyrics. The Victorian successors to the Romantics (most notably Tennyson, Browning, and Matthew Arnold) all produced poems—"Ulysses," "My Last Duchess," and "Dover Beach" immediately spring to mind—that everyone should know. Gerard Manley Hopkins, whose work

---

T. S. ELIOT (1888–1965), was born in St. Louis of a prominent family descended of early New England settlers, and he could trace his lineage back to the Tudor humanist, Sir Thomas

remained unpublished for almost thirty years after his death, was the greatest English devotional poet since Herbert. The first great American poets come late in the nineteenth century: the reclusive spinster Emily Dickinson and the bumptious, self-educated and self-promoting Walt Whitman. William Butler Yeats may well be the greatest poet to write in English in the twentieth century, and I would add Robert Frost, T. S. Eliot, and Wallace Stevens.

Elyot. He went to England and France to complete work on a Harvard Ph.D. dissertation in philosophy, but eventually abandoned philosophy for poetry and never took his degree, settling permanently in England in 1915. The publication of *The Waste Land* in 1922 was one of the seminal events of twentieth-century literature, comparable in its effect to the first performance of Stravinsky's *Rite of Spring* or Picasso's cubist paintings. With this single poem, deploying numerous literary allusions and a dense, difficult stream-of-consciousness technique, Eliot's fame and notoriety were established. He seemed to be mounting a radical attack on the impersonal industrial society from which modern man feels a deep sense of alienation; hence it was a great shock to the intellectual world when, in 1928, having just become a British citizen, Eliot proclaimed himself a classicist in literature, a royalist in politics, and an Anglo-Catholic in religion. Over the succeeding decades he would establish himself as the most important modern literary critic of the English-speaking world and an important conservative commentator on religious and cultural affairs. His efforts to reestablish verse drama in plays like *Murder in the Cathedral* and *The Cocktail Party* have attained, at best, mixed success; however, in works like *Ash Wednesday* and *Four Quartets*, he has offered the finest devotional poetry of our century.

All the authors and works that I have mentioned are worth reading, and every educated man and woman will wish to have at least a passing acquaintance with almost all of them; but of course these are works that require (and repay!) close attention and repeated readings. Still, much of one's reading should be for pleasure, and everyone will have a personal interest in certain books and authors because of sympathy with their religious or ethnic attachments or their philosophical or political views. Such interests ought to be pursued, but all one's reading will be enhanced by a sense of the overall contours of Western literature and by an acquaintance with its greatest monuments. Readers, like authors, need to know where they stand in relation to the past in order to live fully in the present; they need to recognize the genius of others in order to realize their own.

NOTES

1. *Norton Anthology of English Literature*, ed. M. H. Abrams, et al. (New York: Norton, 1986, 5th Ed., II), 864.

2. Wordsworth, "Preface" to *Lyrical Ballads* (1800), in *Wordsworth: Poetical Works*, ed. Thomas Hutchison (London: Oxford University Press, 1969), 737.

3. René Wellek and Austin Warren, *Theory of Literature*, 3rd ed. (New York: Harcourt, Brace & World, 1962), 142–57.

4. There are, to be sure, twentieth-century poems that are quite long, but no one, I think, has ever found a coherent story in Ezra Pound's *Cantos* or David Jones's *Anathémata*.

5. *An Apologie for Poetrie*, in Elizabethan Critical Essays, ed. G. Gregory Smith (London: Oxford University Press, 1904), I, 160.

6. Ibid., 159.

7. Ibid., 156.

8. Eliot, "Tradition and the Individual Talent," in *The Sacred Wood* (London: Methuen, 1920), 47–59.

BIBLIOGRAPHICAL APPENDIX

⅔

T HIS APPENDIX CONSISTS of four parts. The first,
and most important, is a list in alphabetical order by author that comprises all the important primary
works of literature recommended in the text of the essay with a few additional items not mentioned there.
The second part discusses some of the most important
works that established the Western tradition of literary criticism and scholarship along with some of their
most valuable twentieth-century successors. The third
part calls attention to some of the more egregious of-
fenders against literature in the postmodern era, and
the fourth indicates books that have challenged the
postmodernists' current hegemony in academic literary study.

PRIMARY WORKS OF LITERATURE

Penguin Classics and Oxford World's Classics are the
most prolific publishers of great works of literature in
inexpensive paperback editions, and they usually pro-

vide good introductions and notes with reliable translations. Although Penguin and World's Classics are especially good in the area of ancient classical authors, for anyone with even a smattering of Greek and Latin, the Loeb Library editions, published in the United States by Harvard Press, which furnish the original text and a translation on facing pages, are the obvious choice. Norton Critical Editions have for many years published great books in editions featuring reliable texts and translations, along with a useful selection of background materials, both primary and secondary. Recent editions have tended more and more to include secondary essays on the basis of political correctness rather than scholarly or interpretive value (see the Cervantes entry below). Many very fine older Norton editions are, happily, still available.

AESCHYLUS (525/456 B.C.), *Oresteia* (*Agamemnon*; *Libation Bearers*; *Eumenides*). There are numerous fine translations of this trilogy, but Paul Roche's is especially commendable.

ARISTOPHANES (CA. 445–CA. 385 B.C.), *Clouds*; *Frogs*; *Lysistrata*. Benjamin Bickley Rogers is widely regarded as the translator who sets the standard.

MATTHEW ARNOLD (1822–88). A handful of poems, especially "Dover Beach," "The Buried Life," "Empedocles on Etna," and "Thyrsis," are indispensable.

JANE AUSTEN (1775–1817), *Pride and Prejudice*; *Emma*; *Persuasion*.

HONORS DE BALZAC (1799–1850), *Pere Goriot*; *Eugenie Grandet*.

PIERRE AUGUSTIN DE BEAUMARCHAIS (1732–99), *The Barber of Seville*; *The Marriage of Figaro*.

SAMUEL BECKETT (1906–89), *Waiting for Godot*; *Endgame*.

WILLIAM BLAKE (1757–1827), *Songs of Innocence*; *Songs of Experience*. His "prophetical" works are best left to enthusiasts.

GIOVANNI BOCCACCIO (1313–75), *Decameron*.

BERTOLT BRECHT (1898–1956), *Mother Courage and Her Children*; *The Caucasian Chalk Circle*.

ROBERT BROWNING (1812–89), *Men and Women*; *Dramatis Personae*; *The Ring and the Book*.

JOHN BUNYAN (1628–88), *The Pilgrim's Progress*.

GEORGE GORDON, LORD BYRON (1788–1824), *Childe Harold's Pilgrimage*, *Don Juan*.

CALDERON DE LA BARCA (1600–81), *Life Is a Dream*.

CATULLUS (CA. 84–54 B.C.), *Poems*. A superb bilingual edition by Guy Lee is available from World's Classics.

Miguel de Cervantes (1547–1616), *Don Quixote*. Samuel Putnam's translation and notes are still the best. The latest Norton Critical Edition offers a flat and sometimes inaccurate translation by Burton Raffel and a selection of essays emphasizing "gender" and peculiar notions of sexuality.

Geoffrey Chaucer (1340–1400). *The Canterbury Tales* should be read in Middle English. There are numerous good editions that provide adequate help for a diligent student.

Samuel Taylor Coleridge (1772–1834). "The Rime of the Ancient Mariner," "Christabel," "Kubla Khan," the "conversation" poems, and "Dejection: An Ode" are essential.

William Congreve (1670–1729), *The Way of the World*.

Joseph Conrad (1857–1924), *Lord Jim*; *Heart of Darkness*; *Nostromo*; *Victory*.

Pierre Corneille (1606–84), *Le Cid*.

Richard Crashaw (1612/13–1649). Crashaw is notorious for the extravagant conceits of "The Weeper," but the poems to Saint Teresa and the hymns on the Nativity, the Epiphany, and the Holy Name are among the glories of English devotional verse. George Walton Williams's *Complete Poetry of Richard Crashaw* is a model of fine editing.

DANTE ALIGHIERI (1265–1321), *The Divine Comedy.* Allen Mandelbaum's bilingual edition in three inexpensive paperback volumes with good introduction and notes is a remarkable bargain. Charles Singleton's massive three-volume edition is a monument of learning and critical sophistication. Dorothy Sayers's translation is highly esteemed for its commentary.

DANIEL DEFOE (1660–1731), *Robinson Crusoe*; *Moll Flanders.*

CHARLES DICKENS (1812–70), *Bleak House, David Copperfield, Great Expectations.*

EMILY DICKINSON (1830–86). Thomas Johnson's edition of the poems is the standard.

JOHN DONNE (1572–1631). The old-spelling editions of the poems by C. A. Patrides and John Shawcross both have their virtues. A. J. Smith's modernized edition (Penguin) has especially good notes. The Norton Critical Edition by A. L. Clements is extremely useful. Oxford publishes Anthony Raspa's fine edition of the *Devotions upon Emergent Occasions* in paper, and there is a paperback selection of the sermons by Evelyn Simpson, editor of the ten-volume standard edition.

FYODOR DOSTOYEVSKY (1821–81), *Notes from Underground, Crime and Punishment, The Brothers Karamazov.*

JOHN DRYDEN (1631–1700), *Absalom and Achitophel*; *Mac Flecknoe*; *Religio Laici*; *The Hind and the Panther*.

GEORGE ELIOT (MARY ANN EVANS, 1819–80), *The Mill on the Floss*; *Middlemarch*.

T. S. ELIOT (1888–1965). *Selected Poems*, in paperback, contains "The Love Song of J.Alfred Prufrock," "Gerontion," "The Hollow Men," *Ash Wednesday*, *The Waste Land*, and most of the important poems except *Four Quartets*, which is also available in paper, as is *Murder in the Cathedral*, the most important verse drama.

RALPH WALDO EMERSON (1803–1882). *Essays*, first and second series, contain the most important work.

DESIDERIUS ERASMUS (1466–1536). The best translation of *Praise of Folly* is by Clarence Miller, but it lacks the useful background material of Robert M. Adams's fine Norton Critical Edition.

EURIPIDES (CA. 485–CA. 406 B.C.), *Alcestis*; *Bacchae*; *Hippolytus*; *Medea*.

WILLIAM FAULKNER (1897–1962), *The Sound and the Fury*; *As I Lay Dying*; *Absalom, Absalom!*; *Light in August*.

HENRY FIELDING (1707–54), *Joseph Andrews*; *Tom Jones*.

GUSTAVE FLAUBERT (1821–80), *Madame Bovary.*

ROBERT FROST (1874–1963). There are too many fine, characteristically American poems to list. His work is easily accessible and available. His biographers should be ignored.

JOHANN WOLFGANG VON GOETHE (1749–1832), *Faust,* trans. Louis MacNeice.

THOMAS HARDY (1840–1928), *Far from the Madding Crowd, The Return of the Native, Jude the Obscure.*

NATHANIEL HAWTHORNE (1804–1864), *The Scarlet Letter.*

GEORGE HERBERT (1593–1633), *The Temple.* The most useful edition for students is by Louis L. Martz, paired with the poems of Henry Vaughan in the Oxford Authors series.

ROBERT HERRICK (1591–1674). *Hesperides* and *Noble Numbers* are charming secular and sacred poems published together in a fine paperback edition by J. Max Patrick.

HOMER (FL. CA. 700 B.C.). There are superb modern translations of the *Iliad* and the *Odyssey* by Robert Fagles, Robert Fitzgerald, and Richmond Lattimore, but the Elizabethan translation of the *Iliad* by George Chapman and the eighteenth-century translation by Alexander Pope are both currently available in paperback from Princeton and Penguin, respectively, and are well worth perusal.

GERARD MANLEY HOPKINS (1844–89). The Oxford Authors edition by Catherine Phillips and the Penguin edition by W. H. Gardner are both recommended.

HORACE (65–8 B.C.). James Michie's translation of the *Odes* is exceptional, and Palmer Bovie's *Satires and Epistles* is satisfactory. David Ferry's translation of the *Odes* has been met with acclaim.

VICTOR HUGO (1802–85), *Notre-Dame of Paris*; *Les Miserables*.

HENRIK IBSEN (1828–1906), *A Doll's House*; *An Enemy of the People*; *Hedda Gabler*; *Peer Gynt*.

EUGENE IONESCO (1912–44), *The Bald Soprano*; *Rhinoceros*.

HENRY JAMES (1843–1916), *The Portrait of a Lady*; *The Wings of the Dove*; *The Ambassadors*; *The Golden Bowl*.

BEN JONSON (1572–1637), *Volpone*; *The Alchemist*; *The Silent Woman*.

JAMES JOYCE (1882–1941), *Dubliners*; *A Portrait of the Artist as a Young Man*; *Ulysses*.

JOHN KEATS (1795–1821). There are numerous adequate editions. The indispensable poems are the great odes "To a Nightingale," "On a Grecian Urn," and "To Autumn"; the short narrative "The Eve of St. Agnes"; and some of the sonnets, especially "On First Looking into Chapman's Homer."

LUCRETIUS (CA. 94–CA. 55 B.C.), *De rerum natura.*

THOMAS MANN (1875–1955), *Tonio Kroger*; *Death in Venice*; *The Magic Mountain.*

CHRISTOPHER MARLOWE (1564–1593), *The Jew of Malta*; *Edward II*; *Dr. Faustus.*

ANDREW MARVELL (1621–78). There are excellent paperback editions of the poems by George deF. Lord and Elizabeth Story Donno. The former is more generous in attributing disputed poems to Marvell.

HERMAN MELVILLE (1819–91), *Moby-Dick*; *Bartleby the Scrivener*; *Billy Budd.*

JOHN MILTON (1608–74). The Merritt Hughes one-volume edition of the *Complete Poems and Major Prose* is a tremendous bargain. The Longman edition of the poetry by John Carey and Alistair Fowler offers a remarkably thorough commentary.

MOLIERE (JEAN BAPTISTE POQUELIN, 1622–73). Richard Wilbur's translations of *Tartuffe* and *The Misanthrope* are simply superb.

SAINT THOMAS MORE (1478–1535). The most useful edition of *Utopia* for students is the Norton Critical Edition edited and translated by Robert M. Adams. The Penguin edition by Paul Turner attempts injudicious modernization and is nearly unreadable. *A Dialogue of Comfort against Tribulation* is available in paperback from Yale by the editors of the standard Yale edition.

FLANNERY O'CONNOR (1925–64), *A Good Man Is Hard to Find*; *Wise Blood*.

OVID (43 B.C.–A.D. 17). Rolfe Humphries and Horace Gregory have produced excellent verse translations of the *Metamorphoses*, and Guy Lee's bilingual edition of the *Amores* is fine. Peter Green's translation of the *Erotic Poems* (*Amores*, *Art of Love*, etc.) is especially valuable for its introduction and commentary.

FRANCIS PETRARCH (1304–74). Robert M. Durling's *Petrarch's Lyric Poems*, available in paperback from Harvard, provides the original text, lucid prose translations, and a thorough and learned commentary. It is the only choice.

LUIGI PIRANDELLO (1867–1936), *Six Characters in Search of an Author*.

ALEXANDER POPE (1688–1744). *An Essay on Criticism*, *The Rape of the Lock*, *The Dunciad*, and the verse epistles are most important. The one-volume Twickenham Edition, edited by John Butt, is probably the best choice, but there are fine selected volumes edited by scholars like William K. Wimsatt Jr. and Aubrey Williams.

MARCEL PROUST (1871–1922), *Remembrance of Things Past.*

FRANCOIS RABELAIS (1494?–1553), *Gargantua and Pantagruel.*

JEAN RACINE (1639–99), *Phaedra; Andromache.*

SAPPHO OF LESBOS (B. CA. 612 B.C.). The surviving fragments constitute one of the main sources of the love lyric of the Western world.

FRIEDRICH VON SCHILLER (1759–1805). Schiller is most famous for his "Ode to Joy," brilliantly set to music in the final movement of Beethoven's Symphony no. 9. *Wallenstein, Maria Stuart, The Maid of Orleans,* and *Wilhelm Tell* (which inspired Rossini's opera) are important dramas.

WILLIAM SHAKESPEARE (1564–1616). The best complete one-volume edition is the Riverside, general editor G. B. Evans. The Norton Shakespeare combines the problematic Oxford text with a wearisome new historicist commentary. The Arden edition of the plays and poems in individual volumes is rightly regarded as the standard, but the Signet editions are much cheaper and quite satisfactory. The Arden edition of the *Sonnets* by Katherine Duncan-Jones and the Penguin edition by John Kerrigan both feature modernized texts and impressive commentaries. Perhaps the best choice remains Stephen Booth's Yale edition with the editor's modernized version and the 1609 quarto version on facing pages plus an extraordinarily full commentary.

GEORGE BERNARD SHAW (1856–1950), *Saint Joan*; *Arms and the Man*; *Man and Superman*; *Pygmalion*.

MARY WOLLSTONECRAFT SHELLEY (1797–1851), *Frankenstein*.

PERCY BYSSHE SHELLEY (1792–1822), *Prometheus Unbound*; "Ode to the West Wind"; "To a Sky-Lark"; "Adonais."

RICHARD SHERIDAN (1751–1816), *The Rivals*; *The School for Scandal*.

SIR PHILIP SIDNEY (1554–86), *Astrophil and Stella*; *The Countess of Pembroke's Arcadia*.

EDMUND SPENSER (1552–99). The complete *Faerie Queene* is available in a well-annotated paperback edition edited by Thomas Roche. Among the minor poems, the *Shepheardes Calender* is the most important set of pastoral eclogues of the English Renaissance, and the *Amoretti* and *Epithalamion* the finest celebration of courtship and marriage.

LAURENCE STERNE (1713–68), *Tristram Shandy*.

WALLACE STEVENS (1879–1955). *Collected Poems* is available in paperback as well as a generous selection of poetry and prose in *The Palm at the End of the Mind*. The Library of America volume of *Collected Poetry and Prose* is most useful.

JONATHAN SWIFT (1667–745), *A Modest Proposal*; *Gulliver's Travels*; *A Tale of a Tub*.

ALFRED, LORD TENNYSON (1809–92), *In Memoriam*; "Ulysses"; "Tithonus"; "Mariana."

WILLIAM MAKEPEACE THACKERAY (1811–63), *Vanity Fair*; *Henry Esmond*; *The Luck of Barry Lyndon*.

THEOCRITUS (CA. 300–CA. 260 B.C.), *Idylls*.

TIRSO DE MOLINA (1580–1648), *The Joker of Seville*.

J. R. R. TOLKIEN (1892–1973), *The Hobbit*; *The Lord of the Rings*.

LEO TOLSTOY (1828–1910), *Anna Karenina*; *War and Peace*.

ANTHONY TROLLOPE (1815–82), *Barchester Towers*; *The Prime Minister*; *The Way We Live Now*.

IVAN TURGENEV (1818–83), *Fathers and Sons*.

MARK TWAIN (SAMUEL CLEMENS, 1835–1910), *Huckleberry Finn*.

SIGRID UNDSET (1882–1949), *Kristin Lavransdatter*; *The Master of Hestviken*.

HENRY VAUGHAN (1622–95), *Silex Scintillans.*

LOPE DE VEGA (1562–1635), *The Sheep Well; The Foolish Lady.*

VIRGIL (70–19 B.C.). Excellent verse translations of the *Aeneid* by Robert Fitzgerald and Allen Mandelbaum are available in inexpensive paperback editions. Guy Lee's bilingual edition of the *Eclogues* (World's Classics) is perhaps the finest of his superb translations of Latin poets. L. P. Wilkinson has produced a very good translation of the *Georgics* with an excellent introduction and commentary (Penguin).

WALT WHITMAN (1819–92), *Leaves of Grass.*

VIRGINIA WOOLF (1882–1941), *Mrs. Dalloway; To the Lighthouse.*

WILLIAM WORDSWORTH (1770–1850), *The Prelude;* "Lines Composed a Few Miles above Tintern Abbey"; "Ode: Intimations of Immortality"; "Lucy" poems.

WILLIAM BUTLER YEATS (1865–1939), "The Wild Swans at Coole"; "The Second Coming"; "Leda and the Swan"; "Among School Children"; "Sailing to Byzantium"; "Byzantium"; "Under Ben Bulben."

THE CRITICAL AND SCHOLARLY
TRADITION

⁂

LITERARY CRITICISM BEGINS with **Plato** (ca. 429–347 B.C.), whose critique of poetry in the *Ion* and the *Republic* first raises philosophical questions about the form and the ethical and intellectual content of literature. The Symposium and the *Phaedrus* are also especially important for the literary tradition for their discussion of love in its various manifestations (a perennial theme of poets), and the *Phaedrus* and the *Gorgias* for their critique of rhetoric. **Aristotle**'s *Poetics* is the first systematic treatise in literary theory, and it provides a rejoinder to Plato by defending the formal integrity and social utility of poetry. The terms and concepts that Aristotle introduces in the *Poetics* remain at the heart of literary discussion to this day. **Horace**'s *Art of Poetry* (actually *Epistles* 11.3, "Ad Pisones") is both a fine poem and a wide-ranging discussion of poetic issues. *On the Sublime* by "Longinus" is probably not by Cassius **Longinus,** the third-century A.D. rhetorician, but is more safely dated to the end of the first century A.D.

The great tradition of literary criticism in English begins with **Sir Philip Sidney**'s *Apology for Poetry* (or *Defence of Poesie),* which is an intelligent and original rethinking of the Aristotelian/Platonic tradition as it is filtered through the Italian humanist critics of the sixteenth century. **Ben Jonson's** dramatic prefaces and his *Timber, or Discoveries* (an elaborate commonplace book) makes an important contribution, and **John Dryden** initiates the tradition of the critic as man of letters writing to a polite, sophisticated general audience. In addition to the prefaces to his own works, his *Of Dramatic Poesy: An Essay* is especially important. This style of addressing the educated general reader is continued by **Joseph Addison** (1672–1719) and **Richard Steele** (1672–1729) writing in early examples of the cultivated periodical, the *Tatler* and the *Spectator.* **Alexander Pope**'s *Essay on Criticism,* like Horace's *Art of Poetry* on which it is modeled, is both a brilliant poem and a thoughtful discussion of critical issues in literature. **Dr. Samuel Johnson** (1709–84) was the first English lexicographer, a fine poet and essayist, and certainly the greatest critic to write in English. In addition to essays in the *Rambler* and the *Idler,* his best criticism is contained in his great edition of the works of Shakespeare and his *Lives of the Poets.*

The "Preface" composed by **William Wordsworth** for the 1800 edition of *Lyrical Ballads,* a collection of poetry by Wordsworth and Samuel Taylor Coleridge, is the first great English statement of the principles of

Romanticism. The greatest Romantic critic, and one of the greatest of all English critics, is **Coleridge** himself. The most important work is *Biographia Literaria,* but there is also very important critical theory scattered through Coleridge's comments on Shakespeare and seventeenth-century poetry. **Shelley**'s *Defence of Poetry* is a piece of grand critical rhetoric, and the letters of **John Keats** contain a great deal of provocative literary criticism. Although much maligned by the contemporary postmodernist establishment, **Matthew Arnold**, the dominant man of letters of the Victorian era, remains a literary and cultural critic of great insight and judgment. The literary criticism of **G. K. Chesterton** (1874–1936) is unique for its good humor as well as its good sense.

The twentieth century has seen the ascendancy of academic literary criticism written by professors in universities and colleges as opposed to the criticism of poets and men of letters. Of course, many poets and men of letters have found a haven in universities during our time, and for much of the century the great tradition of English literary criticism was maintained in the academic world. I wish to call attention to a few modern critics whom I believe to be particularly useful for students seeking guidance or models in the interpretation and evaluation of literature. There is no pretense of mentioning every important, influential, or valuable critic here, and the selection is largely determined by my own interests and experience.

Despite the academic bias of the past few generations, **T. S. Eliot**, who is in some ways the most important poet of this century, is certainly its most important critic. *Selected Essays* makes a good sample of his literary thought available, including his single most important essay, "Tradition and the Individual Talent." Eliot's poetry and criticism were a principal influence on the American New Criticism, which begins in the Southern Agrarian movement of the 1930s. The poet/critics **John Crowe Ransom** (1888–1974), whose most important work is *The World's Body,* and **Allen Tate** (1899–1979), whose *Essays of Four Decades* has recently been reprinted by ISI (1999), are its most important representatives. A student of Ransom, **Cleanth Brooks** (1906–93), exerted tremendous influence on the teaching of literature by means of introductory anthologies, like *Understanding Poetry* (with **Robert Penn Warren,** 1905–89), as well as on literary scholarship in such works as *The Well Wrought Urn.* At Yale, Brooks was joined by a number of kindred spirits including **René Wellek** (1903–95) and **William K. Wimsatt** (1907–75). Wimsatt collaborated with Brooks on *Literary Criticism: A Short History,* which is a remarkably readable and thorough account of its subject in a reasonably compact format. Wimsatt's collections of essays, *The Verbal Icon, Hateful Contraries,* and *The Day of the Leopards* provide the most sophisticated expositions and defenses of the moral and aesthetic principles of the New Criticism available.

Wellek's collaboration with **Austin Warren,** *Theory of Literature,* is a brilliant epitome of serious thought about the nature and purpose of literature through the middle of the twentieth century.

Among critics who take various theoretical perspectives while providing illuminating commentary both on the nature of literature in general and on the interpretation of specific works, I would especially recommend **M. H. Abrams** (b. 1912: *The Mirror and the Lamp; Natural Supernaturalism);* **Erich Auerbach** (1892–1975: *Mimesis);* **Wayne Booth** (1921–2005: *The Rhetoric of Irony; The Rhetoric of Fiction);* **C. S. Lewis** (1898–1963: *The Allegory of Love; The Discarded Image);* **Maynard Mack** (1920–2001: *Everybody's Shakespeare);* Louis Martz (1915–2002: *The Poetry of Meditation);* and **Lionel Trilling** (1905–75: *The Liberal Imagination; The Opposing Self)* .

THE POSTMODERNIST ASSAULT

The critics mentioned in the preceding section, for all their differences, accept the essential integrity of the literary work of art as a meaningful representation of the reality of moral significance. Since its emergence in the 1960s, a broad movement of reductivism, culminating in the postmodernism of the 1990s, has sought to diminish literature to the status of a mere cultural phenomenon—a product of ideology reducible in theory to its material causes. Although the emergence of postmodernism could be traced back through the entire tortuous history of modern philosophy, with its inception in epistemological doubt, and behind that into medieval nominalism, the immediate philosophical impetus comes from the work of the German philosophers **Friedrich Nietzsche** (1844–1900) and **Martin Heidegger** (1889–1976). Nietzsche, who began his career as a brilliantly original classical philologist, is a forerunner of existentialism, and his later work, as he drifted into madness brought on by syphilis, became increasingly nihilist. Heidegger was a brilliant disciple of the phenomenologist Edmund Husserl, but Heidegger came to regard the entire Western tradition, beginning with Plato, as radically flawed and sought to reconstruct it from the ground up after attempting to obliterate the work of all his predecessors. He was also a Nazi until Hitler's defeat and seems to have remained unrepentant until his death—an embarrassing fact that his adherents have difficulty explaining.

The rather dubious heritage of these German philosophers has become a major factor in literature departments in American universities and colleges largely through the efforts of three Frenchmen: **Jacques Derrida** (1930–2004), **Michel Foucault** (1926–84), and **Jacques Lacan** (1901–81). Sometimes **Roland Barthes** (1915–80) is included in this group, but he has not generally been considered as intellectually profound or influential—probably because his writing is usually free of deliberate obscurity and is not without a certain puckish humor. It is important to note that Derrida's academic training was in philosophy, Foucault's in philosophy and psychology, and Lacan's in psychiatry and psychoanalysis; that is, not one of them is a literary scholar, and yet their influence among English departments in America and Great Britain is immense. The style of these men is difficult by design, and a great deal of the mystique is generated by deploying arcane, coterie jargon, improbable syntax, and acrobatic leaps in logic. With that in mind, the most accessible work by Derrida is *Speech and Phenomena,* which also includes (in the American translation by David Allison) a translation of the important essay, "Writing and Difference." Another important and relatively intelligible essay is "Plato's Pharmacy," which is reprinted in *Dissemination.* Foucault's single most important work is the essay, "What is an Author," reprinted in *The Foucault Reader.* Some sense of what has happened to academic literary study may be perceived by observing that no books are more influential in English departments than Foucault's *History of Sexuality,* his *Discipline and Punish: The Birth of the Prison,* and his *Madness and Civilization.* This preoccupation with sociological history suggests that literary scholars have lost their confidence in literature as a valid field of study in itself. Finally, Lacan has presented a radical revision of Freudian psychoanalysis derived from linguistics, and it is in fact the prominence of language, which is thought to determine mind and mental activity (rather than the other way around), that unites the work of these three men, who seemed to have regarded one another with jealousy and suspicion. Lacan's writing is uniformly impenetrable, but the general idea can be gathered from a selection edited by Juliet Mitchell and Jacqueline Rose, *Feminine Sexuality: Jacques Lacan and the école Freudienne.*

Derrida is the father of **deconstruction**, and his preeminent publicist in this country was **Paul de Man** (1919–83), whose most important work is a heterogeneous collection of essays, *Blindness and Insight.* After his death, de Man was found to have written anti-Semitic articles for a collaborationist newspaper in Nazi-occupied Belgium when he was a young man (is there a pattern here?). De Man was helped out by **Geoffrey Hartman** (b. 1929) and **J. Hillis Miller** (b. 1928); the fourth member of the Yale "Gang of Four" (how things changed at Yale in barely a decade!) was **Harold Bloom** (b. 1930), who offered a robust, Emersonian version of Freud in works like *The Anxiety of Influence: A Theory of Poetry* and *Agon: Towards a Theory of Literary Revisionism.* In recent years he has become what passes for a conservative in contemporary academe by defending Shakespeare and the Western canon. Lacan is most influential among radical feminists like **Julia Kristeva** (b. 1941) and **Jane Gallop,** who maintain that human nature and "gender rôles" are "socially constructed" and have no basis in human nature. The greatest influence by far is now Foucault, whose work is the principal intellectual foundation for **cultural materialism** in Great Britain and the new historicism in America, as well as various offshoots, such as queer theory. New historicism and its various permutations are so pervasive that it is hardly worth attempting to compile a list of the usual suspects—their names are legion. Whenever phrases like "the gendered body as a site of contestation" or "transgressive revisions of the constructed other" appear, it is a sure thing that someone is seeking tenure and promotion. There are also a number of self-designated Marxists still around, like **Terry Eagleton** (b. 1943) in England and **Fredric Jameson** (b. 1934) in America. The latter, an unrepentant defender of Mao Zedong and Stalin, is one of the most widely quoted critics in America. Finally, special mention must be made of **Stanley Fish** (b. 1938), who is rather hard to characterize because his positions keep changing. He glories in the accusation of sophistry, and the only constant in his work is a persistent intellectual and moral relativism, which he calls "antifoundationalism." His only solid commitment is to the power and prestige of the professoriate, which he seems to regard as an end in itself. In fairness, it must be noted that Fish is unusual among contemporary literary critics for the lucidity and liveliness of his style, but the substance of his work is sadly summed up in a recent title: *There's No Such Thing as Free Speech and It's a Good Thing, Too.*

RESPONSES TO POSTMODERNISM

The hegemony (to appropriate a favorite postmodernist term) of postmodernism and political correctness in American higher education in general, and especially in departments of English and foreign languages, is far more total and repressive than is usually acknowledged in the news media or recognized among the general public. Nevertheless, there have been rejoinders. I mention only a few important works that take up the matter from a specifically literary perspective: John M. Ellis, *Against Deconstruction* and *Literature Lost: Social Agendas and the Corruption of the Humanities*; David M. Hirsch, *The Deconstruction of Literature: Criticism After Auschwitz*; David Lehman, *Signs of the Times: Deconstruction and the Fall of Paul de Man*; Stanley Stewart, *Renaissance Talk: Ordinary Language and the Mystique of Critical Problems*; René Wellek, *The Attack on Literature and Other Essays*; and R. V. Young, *At War with the Word: Literary Theory and Liberal Education* (published by ISI).

EMBARKING ON A LIFELONG PURSUIT OF KNOWLEDGE?

⁂

Take Advantage of These Resources

T HE ISI GUIDES to the Major Disciplines are part of the Intercollegiate Studies Institute's (ISI) Student Self-Reliance Project, an integrated, sequential program of educational supplements designed to guide students in making key decisions that will enable them to acquire an appreciation of the accomplishments of Western civilization.

Developed with fifteen months of detailed advice from college professors and students, these resources provide advice in course selection and guidance in actual coursework. The project elements can be used independently by students to navigate the existing university curriculum in a way that deepens their understanding of our Western intellectual heritage. As indicated below, the Project's integrated components will answer key questions at each stage of a student's education.

What are the strengths and weaknesses of the most selective schools?

Choosing the Right College directs prospective college students to the best and worst that top American colleges have to offer.

What is the essence of a liberal arts education?
A Student's Guide to Liberal Learning introduces students to the vital connection between liberal education and political liberty.

What core courses should every student take?
A Student's Guide to the Core Curriculum instructs students in building their own core curricula, utilizing electives available at virtually every university, and discusses how to identify and overcome contemporary political biases in those courses.

How can students learn from the best minds in their major fields of study?
Student Guides to the Major Disciplines introduce students to overlooked and misrepresented classics, facilitating work within their majors.

Which great modern thinkers are neglected?
The Library of Modern Thinkers will introduce students to great minds who have contributed to the literature of the West but are nevertheless neglected or denigrated in today's classroom. Figures in this series include Robert Nisbet, Eric Voegelin, Wilhelm Röpke, Ludwig von Mises, Michael Oakeshott, Bertrand de Jouvenal, and others.

Check out www.collegeguide.org for more information and to access unparalleled resources for making the most of your college experience. ISI is a one-stop resource for serious students of all ages. Visit www.isi.org or call 1-800-526-7022.